About the a

At her family's request, Anne Bolam (née Peterkin), wrote a synopsis of her time as a nurse.

Since writing the book *Don't Drop it, Nurse*, Anne suffered a second stroke, but was determined to finish book two, despite difficulty with her eyesight.

Anne continues to be as active as she can. She enjoys going to church, playing the piano, and spending time with family and friends. Anne also loves being in the company of dogs.

Anne's motto continues to be:
Do the things you are able to do, and forget what you were able to do in the past.

DON'T DROP IT NURSE!

BOOK TWO

With every good wish from
Anne Bolam —Author

ANNE M.G. BOLAM

DON'T DROP IT NURSE!
BOOK TWO

To Leo

Christmas 2017

Love from
Anne!

My 2nd book

Vanguard Press

A CIP catalogue record for this title is
available from the British Library.

ISBN 978 1 80016 433 8

*Vanguard Press is an imprint of
Pegasus Elliot MacKenzie Publishers Ltd.*
www.pegasuspublishers.com

First Published in 2021

**Vanguard Press
Sheraton House Castle Park
Cambridge England**

Printed & Bound in Great Britain

Dedication

I dedicate this book to my dear, late husband, David, who was one of the most tolerant of men. Also to my daughters, Rose and Frances; their husbands, Ken and Rory; and all four of my fabulous grandchildren, Bethany, Naomi, Charlotte and Michael.

I have donated letters and cine film from my time in Aden to the Imperial War Museum.

Book Two: Anne's Life up to Date

As stated, this book has been written as a follow up to book one, *Don't Drop it nurse!* the 'it' referring to the first live kidney transplant in the world performed by Professor Woodruff.

I happened to be the nurse who was delegated to take it between two theatres — not having any idea what was in between the two stainless kidney dishes I was bearing.

Fortunately, I did not drop the kidney, and a successful transplant was performed between twin brothers.

This book has been requested by my family who felt I still had a host of stories to tell.

I wish to give credit to my two daughters, their patient husbands and my four grandchildren who have given me great encouragement.

Introduction

My family and friends have asked me to write a second book with my nursing and other experiences, so this I am endeavouring to do.

As I leave my bedroom I glance round the room and on a bedside table, see two books that have been very important to me as I travel through life, for they have come with me wherever I go.

The first was given to me by my grandfather, Reverend Hugh Elder when I was baptised by him on 31st July 1938 in Mayfield North Church, Edinburgh. It is a St James Bible, authorised edition in which is inscribed by Grandad, Psalm 119 verse 105.

The second book was given to me by my grandmother, his wife, and is called *Come Ye Apart*. The teachings of Jesus. I was a child then. I carried each book with me wherever I travelled.

I had a very happy childhood and enjoyed the company of my brother and sister. We did go to Sunday school where it was expected that each child would do a party piece at the Christmas party. For example, at one party, my sister and I were very demure and I quoted *The Lamb* by William Blake. My sister played a piece on the piano, and my brother who would not tell anyone what he was doing quoted, "Father heard his children scream so he threw them in the stream, saying as he drowned the third 'Children should be seen, not heard'." The poor minister was quite shaken as he had no children.

My sister and I were apparently disgusted at our younger brother's antics.

Chapter One
Further Childhood Memories

My father returned from the war and as well as part of his uniform, much to our delight, brought a green canvas basin bucket and bath with him. My sister and I, thought this was fantastic, and scrubbed the old coal cellar we had outside the back door. It had a wide shelf in it, so we made a bed. This was to accommodate tramps and homeless folk. Much to our mother's chagrin we put a large notice on the front gate which said 'Free accommodation — Tramps welcome'.

It was duly pointed out to us that it wasn't suitable as there was no toilet. We did point out that we didn't mind them sharing the toilet in the house. We were encouraged to use it as a playhouse and had great fun playing in it with our dolls etc.

The years rolled happily by and Mother and Father used to start going out together. They had a babysitter called Margaret who was left in charge of us. She had strong orders not to bring *Broon* into our home. *Broon* (Brown) had been in the Glasshouse in the army for an unknown punishment and had been discharged from the army. I came down to the kitchen for a drink of water and found Margaret and Broon making fake money.

They had a fluorescent lamp and a sort of mini mangle and were churning out £1 notes. I was chased up to bed and informed it was "our secret".

I kept the secret for about two weeks, until I heard my mother saying she was going to the bank to get some money and I told her there was no need. The Edinburgh Police wondered where all the fake money circulating in Edinburgh was coming from.

I was about eight years old at that time.

Chapter Two
More Childhood Days

It was lovely to have our dad home after the war. My sister Alison and I went to St George's school for girls. Initially, we walked, I am told it was five miles across country past the Hearts football training ground and took two trams home to the other side of Edinburgh. Dad very kindly offered to drive us to school in the morning as it was on his way to work at his consulting rooms. As young adults he told us his morning smile was seeing a wartime poster at Haymarket Station which said 'Stamp out Venereal Disease' and a smiling lady saying 'I got it at the Co-op'.

While my sister and I wended our way to St Georges, our brother Bill had an interview at the local school. He was asked how many buttons he had on his jacket and said, "Far too many." It was decided that after a preliminary time at George Watson's, he should be entered for Clifton Hall — a boys prep school outside Edinburgh. He started there at the age of eight years old.

Holidays and weekends passed in a lovely haze of childhood, interspersed with piano lessons taken by an elderly lady known as Aunty Ann. She lived at the top of a tenement and thought nothing of whacking our knuckles with a cane. My parents felt sorry for her at Christmas as she was on her own, so Dad would put on some family slides alternating with horrible pictures of skin diseases. As children, we thought this was great.

During the war my father made many American friends and I can remember him having a trip out there and bringing us back lovely summer dresses and I was given a sweet little papoose which I wore as a brooch. He brought my brother a Slinky toy which would slide up and downstairs.

My brother settled in well to prep school and at parent's evening were informed that his favourite hobby was frightening lovers on Craiglochart Hill. He and a friend, armed with cap pistols and alarm clocks, would find American sailors who had taken girls into the hill behind our home and frightened the poor souls plus-plus. I believe the teacher and my parents were duly shocked, but also had wry smiles on their faces.

Chapter Three
Family Holidays

We had wonderful childhood holidays and our parents took us up to Aviemore or Rothiemurchus where we enjoyed lovely Highland walks. I can still recall the wonderful smell of the wood fires and the scent of newly mown hay. We normally had a dog with us, and how he enjoyed running all over the place and smelling the wild animals. It was not unknown for him to chase a deer, but he never managed to catch one.

We usually went on holiday by car or train. I remember once getting stuck in a ford and being pulled out by a farmer with his Clydesdale horses. The river water had come right into the car. Great excitement. One of my favourite places was Loch Morlich where we enjoyed playing in a rubber dinghy and swimming. We took a young doctor called Peter Smith with us and my sister Alison was heard to say, "Oh Peter, fancy coming round this way when I have my knickers on back to front."

Dad took us walking up Cairngorm Mountain. I can still remember my brother looking in vain for a Cairngorm stone (jewel). He was only six years old and we sisters rather cursed that he held us up. He did get to the top though.

We normally went to the Cairngorms in the summer, that included me doing a spot of pony trekking. I did try my hand at skiing in the winter when we had quite a bit of snow. However, skiing is not my cup of tea.

It was lovely to return to our lodgings and have a heavenly warm bath. The water was brown, due to the peat in the soil.

The colours of the forests and mountains were magnificent and we all ate a hearty meal due to the wonderful air which gave us fantastic appetites.

Chapter Four
Teenage years

At the age of fifteen, I was still determined to be a nurse and secured a voluntary job in a local mother and baby home during the holidays and on a Saturday. I loved this job and preferred it to going to school.

At this point I became very religious and avidly read *On the edge of the Primeval Forest* by Albert Sweitzer. He was a missionary doctor who took his grand piano into the forest. He was a magnificent organ player and I still have some of his records. I read about Mary Slessor of Calabar, Hudson Taylor of the Chinese Inland Mission and others. There was a Mau Mau uprising in Kenya at the time.

I tried to persuade my mother to let me go and try and convert the Mau Mau to Christianity. She advised me that I ought to do my nurses training first. Undeterred, I packed a small case and trotted down to see our minister, Reverend George Campbell, who was very kind and understanding and fortunately agreed with my mother.

I settled down to my O levels after this, which I sat at the age of sixteen and got enough to start my nursing career at seventeen.

To fill in time till I could start my career I spent six weeks in France looking after two small boys in Versailles. Pansy, the mother had done her nurses training in Edinburgh where my parents were very good to her. During the war, Guernsey was cut off by the Germans where Pansy's father was. Dean, Pansy's husband was a teacher in Troyes, France and was trying to earn some money for them.

When I returned home, I learned that my cousin Peter, at the age of two, had developed a Wilms tumour which travelled to his lung at the age of four. He had a nanny who needed some time off, so I relieved her. I became very close to his elder brother who sadly was born with club feet, so I learned how to put his special boots on — Dennis Brown Boots. Peter's parents were very kind to me and took me to London, Windsor etc.

They lived in a school in Northwood. When Nanny came back it was time for me to return to Edinburgh and start my nurses training.

Chapter Five
Start of Nurses Training

My first book mentions my training in Edinburgh at the Princess Margaret Rose Hospital.

This was a rural hospital catering for patients suffering from TB. I can remember pushing the beds outside in all weathers. Some poor souls had snow on their covers. We used to have to give Streptomycin injections and very flat tablets called INAH, normally given with milk.

In those days some patients were sent to Switzerland as it was thought the air there was lovely for those with bad chests.

As we were an orthopaedic hospital, we catered for everything orthopaedic. I remember we opened an adult wing. As I was very young my father told me to throw a cold flannel if a male patient got very fresh. I got a flannel with lots of fingers which I filled with ice cubes. The patient screamed and the consultant had him removed from the ward, traction and all. The consultant said he was not having patients interfering with his young nurses.

I loved nursing the orthopaedic children but as I grew more senior I was moved to two wards called 'the huts'. They had been built during the war to accommodate wounded military personnel.

In those days we had to wash and iron the bandages. While unrolling the bandages off the bathroom radiator I heard the bathroom door become locked. To my horror, a spotty-faced nineteen-year-old patient, pushed me into the bath and tried to rape me. Fortunately, my senior nurse came back from her supper and rescued me. I think the police were called.

That was hut two. Beside it was hut one where a Barnardo's boy we nicknamed, Ginger, had us running round in circles. He used to hide at the top of the airing cupboard and throw blankets on top of us.

I was glad to get back into the main hospital again.

Chapter Six
The Royal Infirmary

The Princess Margaret Rose Hospital was built outside Edinburgh near the Pentland Hills. It was thought to be a healthy environment for TB patients.

By contrast the RIE, as we nicknamed it, was built on Lauriston Place in the centre of Edinburgh. The sluices were in the turrets and I can remember cleaning bedpans there and seeing a man step on to the zebra crossing without looking. A hearse was waiting to pass over the crossing and promptly lifted the injured man into the back and took him straight to casualty round the corner.

On a Saturday evening, or festival evening we had quite a few drunks come in. One of my jobs was to give each one a black coffee enema. This was given by an orange rubber tube up the backside, and poured down a funnel attached to the tube. The men slept it off, sobered up and were shown the door. The smell of black coffee remained with me for years.

On one of the wards there was quite a strict ward sister. She asked a young nurse to give Mr Brown a bed bath and to make sure his umbilicus was well washed as it was very dirty. He told her to, "Look in his locker," to no avail, then said, "Remember, nurse, the wife took it home to wash last night." I was present when the young nurse tried to explain she hadn't been able to wash the umbilicus. She was just out of training school and had forgotten what it was!

Chapter Seven
Peace and Quiet

When I came off duty at the RIE I felt the need to go and have a time of quiet in the chapel. There were several regulars there, so we had a time of fellowship.

I can remember a lovely couple on one of the surgical wards. He had cancer in his lower abdomen and was only twenty-nine years old. I can remember him being in dreadful pain. Unfortunately, we did not have the drugs to give him in those days. His sweet wife spent ages showing him holiday brochures. As far as we knew he would not be going on holiday. She decided it was best if he was not told.

On a male ward there was a lovely old man called the Reverend John Baird. He was eighty-four and was very deaf and blind. He had cancer and because he was very restless, trying to undo his cot sides etc. we had to put soft bandages on his hands. At 0600 hours on Christmas morning the nurses came into the ward singing carols. They sang *O come all ye faithful*. I was on night duty and gently held my patient's hands. Although he was deaf and blind, he joined in the singing of that well known carol. I felt his hands go limp as he peacefully died.

As usual the nurses turned their red capes round for Christmas, showing off their tartans.

I will never forget that Christmas as a nineteen-year-old student nurse!

Chapter Eight
Operating Theatres at the Royal Infirmary Edinburgh

I have never been fond of operating theatres as I always liked to have first-hand knowledge of the patients who to me are people. I can remember cleaning and preparing the instruments also getting the drums full of dressings ready and sterile for the operations. I always felt that the large autoclaves might blow up at any time. I can remember a surgeon shouting, "Mop, nurse, mop, nurse." One of my colleagues rushed and brought him a large floor mop. He of course, wanted his brow mopped.

Once I was a scrub nurse in theatre. This meant picking up anything that had fallen, such as swabs, instruments etc. I had a very bad-tempered surgeon in theatre when it was my turn to be scrub nurse. He threw a scalpel which just missed me as I sat under the table, collecting the instruments. I was not the only nurse to have been assaulted in that way.

That evening my father had some doctors around to our home for a meeting. The bad-tempered surgeon happened to be there, and with his usual charm said to my father, "I don't believe I have met your lovely daughter before." To his amazement, I stated that he had just missed me with a scalpel while I was waiting patiently under the operating table that day. He was well known in the hospital for his temper and the way he treated the nurses. I think that he was so embarrassed that particular evening, I don't recall him ever throwing instruments again, much to the amazement of the nursing and other staff.

In future I had great pleasure tying up his operating gowns too tightly.

Chapter Nine
Midwifery and Orthopaedics

I decided it was time I learned to deliver a baby as I felt it was necessary for a qualified nurse to be able to do this.

As I had done my nurses training in Edinburgh and the Simpson's Maternity hospital seemed to be the place, as Maggie Myles had written the bible about midwifery and she was based in Edinburgh I felt I could apply for Oxford and buy the book.

I thoroughly enjoyed my time in Oxford, although it was a sad time as I delivered two Thalidomide babies. (The drug was also Distaval and was given to mums who had sickness in pregnancy.) I got very friendly with a pregnant girl's mother. The patient had moved away from her usual address to have the baby in secret. She apparently had been date-raped. I had a day off when the girl went into a very difficult labour. On my return, her mother's hair had gone snowy white, possibly due to the stress. The baby was adopted.

As my part two midwifery paperwork had gone missing, I was not too upset as my first love had always been orthopaedic nursing.

I applied to the Nuffield Orthopaedic (Wingfield Morris Hospital) and learned about the wonders of the iron lung.

Mary Marlborough Lodge, a rehabilitation ward was part of my time at the Nuffield Orthopaedic Hospital. The engineers were experimenting with toilets that could clean and dry the patients. Two of us volunteered, with the doors shut. I found myself shooting into the air with the water spray and the doctors, physios, occupational therapists, laughing at my expense. Recently I have been talking to my elder daughter who mentioned the wonders of these toilets. She is a trained occupational therapist and was amazed to think that her mother was one of the pioneers in the trials.

As I had been acting sister while my colleague was in Australia, Matron offered me a night sister's post. I felt at twenty-four I was too young to become a permanent sister and wanted to see life abroad, so left and joined the PMRAFNS — Princess Mary's Royal Airforce Nursing Service.

I spent a few weeks nursing at the Officer's Nursing Home in Edinburgh until it was time to join up. Matron was called Miss Gunn and the edifice was hence called, 'The Gun Club'.

Chapter Ten
Princess Mary's Royal Airforce Nursing Service

After my interview in London, I was accepted into the PMRAFNS. I can remember there was a mixed bag of folk at the interview. One girl who kept sniffing told us all she was joining up for was to get a man. She did not pass the interview.

I wanted to work with the artificial kidney unit. My father had been in the army and had told me I would be best to join the RAF for the experience. At that time there was an artificial kidney unit at RAF Halton. At the same time, I had an interview with the Rennie's mill orphanage in China. I did not get that job as the vacancy was filled.

In December 1964 I found myself at RAF Halton. It was snowing outside and unfortunately, I lost one of my contact lenses in the snow. A platoon of young RAF men was marching by and one chap gamely found the lens buried in the snow.

My first ward after my posting was the orthopaedic ward.

Sister was dying to have her weekend off and left me in charge to organise Lac Saunders to polish the toilets with cardinal red polish. I thought this was to do the seats with, in order to make them smart for the commanding officers visit the following Monday. That week we had lots of queries from the laundry. The pyjama trousers were bright red!

We normally had lectures during the week and spent the weekends on the wards. I can remember doing square bashing on the parade ground with a SNCO who had a very powerful voice. We girls were not very good at it.

Chapter Eleven
RAF Hospital Ely

I was transferred to the RAF Hospital at Ely after my time at RAF Hospital Halton. This was a female surgical ward with many patients admitted from Addenbrookes Hospital Cambridge to relieve the NHS waiting list. This did include patients in oxygen tents which was very good experience for me.

I remember removing the enormous sutures from a lady's abdominal wound and asking if she wanted to take them home. She asked what she should do with them and I suggested that as her husband was a fisherman, she could give them to him and he could use them as bait. Of course, I was teasing her, but a few weeks later I received a letter, very badly spelt, which said he had the best catch ever!

Naturally, I was very surprised and amused.

I had been there a few weeks when our matron shouted along the corridor, "Peterkin and Grant you are both posted to Aden!" We looked at each other bemused. "Where is Aden?" we questioned. We did not have a clue, but we did find ourselves going there!

Chapter Twelve
Travelling to Aden

There was a nursing sister at RAF Ely who was very anti-church and anti-Christ. Four of us used to go to church regularly and she made fun of us. Anyway, we stood our ground and much to my surprise she leaped into an RAF vehicle and came down to the station to say good bye to me like an old buddy.

I started learning to play the organ at the parish church, Ely but was half asleep when I woke up during the day having gone to bed after a stint on night duty. The organist was gorgeous, about the same age as me and I ticked him off for playing footsie. In fact, the poor soul was trying to teach me the foot pedals. As you can imagine, we were both very embarrassed. He was going to teach me on the Ely Cathedral organ but thank goodness, I was posted to Aden, sparing more embarrassment.

The time came for me to go to Gatwick Airport. I discovered I was travelling on a very full plane. Close to me was a young RAF wife who was going to join her husband overseas. She had very young twin babies and a very restless toddler. I felt very sorry for her and being on my own, offered to help her. I love babies so it was a pleasure for me to take up her eager offer. Travel cots were provided for the babies. They hung from the ceiling.

After we had been in the air for about an hour, we had to ditch the aircraft fuel as there was a problem and return to Gatwick. We were bussed to Brighton and stayed in a posh hotel. I had a lovely en suite bedroom.

Chapter Thirteen
Arriving in Aden

After a long flight when we stopped over at Bahrain, where I was fascinated to see locals with carpets over their shoulders, we arrived in Aden.

I continued to help the poor lady with her babies. She must have felt exhausted after all the travelling. The air hostesses were very helpful in spite of being hectically busy.

On opening the door of the aircraft, it was like walking into a greenhouse, it was so hot, although it was December and the cool season. I was glad to have a summer dress to change into and to reach my room, which was air conditioned.

The evening I arrived there was a Christmas party going on. The gates were guarded by Arab soldiers on camels dressed in official wear. I was invited to stay and in spite of being very tired decided to join the fun.

The following day I was taken on a tour of the hospital and shown the usual admin. There were eight of us nursing sisters in post at the time, there were also a few civilian staff nurses to support us.

The hospital in those days was quite small and catered for solders of the Arab Protectorate and their families.

Britain was pulling out of Aden in those days and as well as British nursing staff, we had Somali personnel helping us. The lowest Arab staff were the Sweepers who swept the floors, cleaned the toilets, did any rough work.

We had to 'watch our backs' the whole time!

Chapter Fourteen
Introduction to Life at Khormaksar Beach Hospital

On the first day I was introduced to our very friendly caring Matron, Doreen Francis. I thought that at forty-two years of age she was ancient. She had a very loud voice and we could hear her by leaving our telephone on the desk when she phoned us. We nicknamed her Fog Horn. I became very friendly with matron who stayed several times with me, and another sister, Alma Tyack (Barnard), when we returned home. We were asked by her nephew to do the eulogy at her funeral in the Methodist Church Rustington.

My first ward was the Female ward at KBH (Khormaksar Beach Hospital). In my first book I have recounted many stories about patients that happened there.

Having come from the sterile NHS, it was difficult to treat patients who got straight up after major spinal surgery. They kept walking round the ward. I remember doing a lumbar puncture with a doctor and a cat sitting on the bed. No hygiene at all!

My next ward was the male medical ward. If we wanted rid of the visitors, I used to call out that we needed blood donors, they soon dispersed!

It was important to recall that most of the patients needed half the dose of medicines that we would have. They also had a reduced diet of food, and used one hand for eating and the other for toilet purposes. We had to be careful which hand we put any tablets into. They had great tureens of rice provided. I can recall patients shouting out if I put tablets into the wrong hand.

I remember a wee boy I nicknamed Oxfam. He weighed eleven and a half pounds, was five years old, and found his way to my room one day. He was wearing nothing but a sunhat. He was so skinny, he was hard to cuddle. The women were mostly very anaemic, after years of childbirth and insufficient food.

It was a privilege to look after these folk.

Chapter Fifteen
Off Duty in Aden

At about this time I was introduced to Dr Fawdry who was the civilian doctor attached to the Queen Elizabeth the large civilian hospital. He was also very involved with the local missionaries. Over a cup of coffee, he introduced me to Gerda Larsen who taught at the Danish Mission school. He was very kind and realised that Gerda was the same age as me (the youngest of all missionaries) and she needed some company of her own age. She was much more glamorous than I imagined a missionary to be and painted her nails red. We immediately struck up a friendship that has lasted till this day. That day I went to my room to find I had been invited to a missionary prayer meeting up country.

This was the beginning of going every Friday afternoon when I was free to a different missionary meeting. The first one I attended was the Red Sea mission team where folk were all dressed in longies (Arab costumes). I ended up playing four hymns on their keyboard and sitting on an orange box as they had no proper furniture. The keyboard player was away that week, so Gerda kindly put me forward to play. There was no time to be nervous. I also had a friend Una who was a nurse at the mission hospital, Shaik Othman. She and I had both nursed in Edinburgh. The doctor who founded the hospital was a Muslim and his father built a mosque the day he opened his hospital. He was apparently dragged through the streets. I also am still in contact with Una who lives in Edinburgh. I learned a great deal from my two missionary friends.

Chapter Sixteen
Men's Ward

After about a year we built the European wing, as the acute hospital at Steamer Point was getting hectically busy with casualties due to the escalating security situation. We looked after men only and the patients were nursed by British boys, with the Arabs and Somali folk doing the cleaning.

I can recall a West Indian soldier who had lost a limb. He screamed and cried and cried. I realised then, that different cultures dealt with things in various ways. The British had stiff upper lips, which was not always good for them to bottle things up. Nowadays we are watching for post-traumatic stress.

One afternoon I was off duty and went to get a bus to the beach with another nursing sister. Like typical nurses we were busy and got off duty late. The bus had just left and was blown up by the terrorists. Fortunately, no one was badly injured.

I decided after that I would buy a small car which might be safer. I shared a green Austin A35 with another sister, Heather Grant. The car was known as the PW, or Passion Wagon.

Our boyfriends were based near the beach and said they reckoned they did not need a car.

Some of the patients got very bored so offered to service the car, which was great. I bought them a darts board and challenged them to a game when I wasn't too busy. To their surprise I beat them as I was a champion in the officer's mess, unbeknownst to them. We also made a snow scene on a large white sheet with skiers made of pipe cleaners.

One evening we sisters were sitting outside the officers Mess having coffee after dinner when a bomb went off thirty yards away from the guard room. Instead of going under the table as we should have done, we sat rigidly, not wanting to break the Nori Taki china we had purchased that afternoon.

Fortunately, no British folk were injured. I believe the terrorists had a few injuries.

Chapter Seventeen
Bombs and Shrapnel

I can remember coming off duty at about nine p.m. to hear a bomb go off. It was all hands on deck. I was in charge of the hospital as one of the matrons was on holiday in Kenya and the other was in UK on compassionate leave. The Commanding Office was also away leaving the senior surgeon in charge of the hospital. He was only thirty-seven years old, I recall. We sisters had to intubate folk, put drips to save lives and had no time to think about what we were doing. I think we had twelve patients in casualty that evening. I got to bed about 0300 hours, then on duty again at 0700 hours.

Another evening I was in casualty and three trollies came in with men lying on their tummies. A brothel had been formed in the town of Maalla and the terrorists had thrown grenades at those using the brothel. We discovered that this had been set up while chaps were up country and that some of the wives left behind were being used. The military police had to be called in.

I was in the ward one day when a patient excitedly told me he'd got married in Mombasa. That day I was in the shower listening to the radio and heard a wife say she was on her way to visit her Darling John. I pelted back to the ward and asked him if he was a bigamist. He went scarlet and I had to get his CO involved to get the second marriage annulled.

Life was never dull in Aden.

Chapter Eighteen
Miscellaneous Events

I can recall having a young guardsman come in with a broken leg and he assured me that he had fallen down a manhole where the cover was off. I could not remember seeing manholes anywhere in Aden. The following day two military policemen came in wanting to interview him. Apparently, the soldier was supposed to be on duty when a woman of debatable age invited him in for some nooky. In his excitement he fell off the roof of the NAAFT. Hence his admission to hospital.

Off duty I had plenty to occupy me, although at one time I felt very homesick and prayed to God that he would give me a purpose in life when I was off duty. I was then asked if I would help with the six to twelve year old club, on a Monday afternoon. It was run by the church. I had Monday afternoon off and found it very fulfilling.

I also helped to run the church coffee shop, and played the harmonium. For the evening service I joined ALOS, the Aden Light Opera Association. So God had plenty for me to do as well as nursing. I joined the Officers' Christian Union which met every week in a different military home. I met my soul mate, David, there. He was an RAF dentist. His friend Clive (equipment Branch) RAF. As good friends, we enjoyed going around in a foursome. The four of us had some wonderful times together and I was bridesmaid at their wedding and Clive was best man at our marriage. We are godparents to each other's daughters.

Chapter Nineteen
Saying Goodbye to the Missionaries

As the terrorists took more and more control of the whole area of Aden, it was sad to see:

1. The Danish Mission burned down. That meant that my friend Gerda had to return to Denmark. The mission was in an area called Crater, which is where the prison was. I have taken some cine film of the well-known Colonel 'Mad Mitch' Mitchell sorting out the terrorists in that area.

2. The mission hospital was also burned down, and Una my friend had to return to Scotland. Her staff were reemployed to my ward, which mercifully at that time was an Arab ward.

The staff would come to my ward in the morning and that evening I would take them in my car to a quiet house the missionaries had acquired, and they had Bible study etc., there. It was quite a dangerous operation as there was a curfew and I had to drive among enemy lines. It would have been much riskier had I been a man.

The terrorists seemed to ignore women. Our drugs were also used for some of the patients.

I felt sorry for those who were ill up country as we used to pass on the drugs for TB, Leprosy etc. One of the soldiers on the adult wing nicked the used syringes and apparently went up country pretending to be a doctor (Hakim).

I felt sad to see the lovely Danish school and bookshop go up in flames. Also, the mission hospital in Sheikh Othman had some lovely memories. I used to visit Una and we would have tea together.

Chapter Twenty
Time to Leave Aden

It was very sad that the Arabs wished us to leave Aden. Some poor souls did not have the intelligence to see that the NAAFI was run by the British and that there were no jobs for them there or in the RAF hospitals. I felt very concerned for them, as that meant there was no money coming in.

The Ayas (nursing staff) gave me a wonderful party when I left with some beautiful silk material to make a dress. I had already attended an Arab wedding, where the ladies were separate from the men. It was a Muslim wedding. I was given some very sweet tea.

My boyfriend, David's duty finished in Aden one year before mine, and bless him he was so keen I received a hundred letters from him and so looked forward enormously to seeing him on my return, though I felt very conscious stricken leaving Aden and returning to a comfortable lifestyle in Great Britain.

Chapter Twenty-one
Returning to the UK

As my tour finished in September 1966 it was time to return to the UK and I travelled with Heather, my friend.

David, my boyfriend and his friend Clive, Heather's boyfriend were at Gatwick to meet us at 0300 hours. What a reunion!

I stayed with David's parents overnight, who I met then for the first time. The next day I travelled to Edinburgh to stay with my lovely family, who were of course glad to see me back safely as they had been worried about the press reports of the terrorism in Aden. The British pulled out in 1967.

After a short time, I went on holiday with David and we got engaged on the Settle to Carlisle Railway at Horton on Ribblesdale and bought my lovely yellow sapphire engagement ring in Skipton. He was a very keen railway enthusiast and spent time keeping the line open, by attending hearings at Appleby and Skipton. British Rail wanted to knock down the Ribblehead viaduct as it was said to be too expensive to maintain. Now the route from Leeds to Carlisle is very busy and is used as a main route to Scotland when the west and east coasts are being maintained.

David and I got married on 21st October 1967, and had a lovely honeymoon by train to the south coast of Italy, even swimming in the sea at Positano.

On our return we found a bungalow to rent at Purley-on-Thames and I started work as relief district nurse locally, and David as a community dentist in Reading.

I joined the Thames Vale singers and we sang anything from Bach, to Gilbert & Sullivan. There was a very active Drama group and we played anything from pantomime to murder mystery plays. I also played the organ in Purley-on-Thames and various churches round the Deanery. David was fire officer and door keeper at the various events. He was also on the Deanery Synod and the Purley Church Council.

We were very happy in our rented bungalow and eventually had two daughters — Rosemary and Frances. Sadly, when my mother died, France was eight weeks old, and Rosemary was three and a half years old. Mum died in February, aged sixty-seven and our lovely rector Reverend Derek Taylor came to do a bereavement visit.

Mothering Sunday was in March and he had heard that I could play the piano. He tentatively wondered if I could help. I said I wondered if I could play the organ so I would be hidden from the congregation in case I was upset.

I went down and taught myself the organ with my baby daughter in a carrycot. My mother had been a beautiful organist and I heard her Scottish voice say,

"The mantle has now fallen on you." I played at Purley for forty years. The first hymn we had that day was *Immortal Invisible* sung at my mother's funeral. I do believe God had a message for me that day!

After that we settled down to family life, with occasional visits to my bereaved father, in Edinburgh.

When the girls reached playgroup and school age I went back to work again as a part time relief district nurse.

In 1980 I remember a caring GP called me into his surgery to ask if I minded nursing a patient with AIDS and I said it was part of my job. Sadly, my colleague was frightened in case she caught it and refused. I had to dress up in a white trouser suit and be very careful to sterilise all the equipment used. I was worried in case the dog bit me and I contracted AIDS. The patient was a very pleasant man whose partner was from Ireland and looked after him very well. They were both so grateful that I was non-judgemental. The patient died peacefully. I believed I nursed the first patient with AIDS in the community in Reading. Today things have certainly moved on and AIDS does not have the stigma it used to have as there are new drugs all the time. I felt sorry for those patients with haemophilia who were given blood transfusions and contracted AIDS. Covid-19 seems to have taken its place with the fear and uncertainty there is with the disease. Thank goodness for vaccinations!

After four years relieving at the same practice — the GPs offered me a twenty-hour week job which my nurse manager said I was not entitled to, as I did not have the district nurse's certificate. Undeterred, as the children were older, I applied and was accepted by Reading University for the full-time course.

Chapter Twenty-two
University Life in Reading

I attended the course to enable me to be a proper district nurse and met some lovely colleagues. Most were much younger that I was but we all learned by experience and inexperience. We students were all given a railcard and had admission to the university library. We also had a practical work teacher who mentored us when we went out on the district. Mine was a lovely lady called Anne Fraser. We still phone each other most days.

After I finished my course, I was appointed to Burdwood Surgery Thatcham. It was a new surgery and I was the first district nursing sister to be appointed there.

Every day I took my lunch to Thatcham, the main surgery, to join my colleagues. We covered each other's work, so at weekends I could cover the patients of three surgeries, Thatcham, Burdwood, Chapel Row. Every month we would have a pub lunch at a pub near where we lived. My colleagues' names were, Anne, Daphne, and Dilys. Sadly, Dilys died a few years ago. We were all strong Christians and enjoyed working with each other and continue to connect to each other by phone, though we are retired.

One day, I was getting ready to take my sandwiches to Thatcham Surgery when a chap came in and was in a terrible state. He had been on the *Herald of Free Enterprise* Ferry and had been a bridge as passengers tried to leave the doomed ferry. He had nightmares the previous night and I reckoned he was suffering from post-traumatic Stress disease, which I had seen in Aden. As soon as I could, I managed to get him an appointment with a GP who was grateful for my diagnosis as he had not had a case before.

Chapter Twenty-three
Up to Date Completion of Journeys

I loved my vocation as a district nurse and it was like a bereavement when I had to take early retirement as the result of a back injury when a heavy patient fell on top of me.

I was fortunate to obtain a twenty-hour week job as a school nurse. Unfortunately, the small chairs and heavy instruments and helping to care for elderly in-laws became too painful for my back.

The Royal College of Nursing were fantastic and got me a job with the Medical Advisory Service answering patients' queries from home by telephone. This helpline was set up to give work-injured and disabled nurses a job and a small income.

My boss was fantastic and put me forward for another job, which she knew I was not keen on as David was talking about retirement. This was to start a medical helpline for retired diplomats at the foreign office. Two doctors had applied so I was sure I would not get it. My husband told me to go for the interview as I couldn't lose anything. To my amazement I was offered the post and enjoyed it for five years.

At the same time, I enjoyed working for SSAFA and the RBL. (Soldiers, Sailors, Airforce and the Royal British Legion). It was a privilege to serve men, women and their families who perhaps needed financial help, a new bed, food, help with housing, a new cooker or washing machine. I served SSAFA for twenty years.

Unfortunately, poor David sustained a bad brain haemorrhage in the garden, so although he recovered well, we decided to move nearer to one of the girls' family as I was finding it hectic looking after David and travelling to Buckinghamshire to help Frances with our grandchildren.

We found a lovely bungalow in Holmer Green about ten minutes from Frances. David loved the garden and the locality.

Because he was feeling very tired, he was given a pacemaker and was found to have leukaemia. He kept reasonably well, and when he was in remission, it was decided by my orthopaedic surgeon, I should have an operation to enable me to look after him in the future. Unfortunately, two operations went wrong and I've ended up with a Caudo Equinovarus which I have been told is a very rare complication after back surgery. Poor David ended up looking after me. He went downhill very quickly and died in Stoke Mandeville Hospital in September 2017. We gave him a wonderful send off in church. He died three weeks before our golden wedding anniversary, which was five weeks after our lovely dog Lucky had to be put to sleep, at the age of fifteen.

In 2018 while having a respite holiday I had a stroke in Worthing.

I have two wonderful daughters, their husbands and four caring grandchildren, and now live in a sheltered flat with twenty-four-hour care.

I am very grateful to the local Baptist church who have made me very welcome, especially at the Life Spring meetings on a Tuesday evening.

I feel so blessed to have such a lovely family and kind friends who have kept me and my husband going over the past difficult years. A special thanks to Jenny who looked after us both and had Lucky the dog in her home with her family.

I am fortunate to have my Christian faith and believe that life is full of chapters which should be grabbed with both hands before they disappear.

Edinburgh Tattoo at the Princess Margaret Rose Hospital,
August 1956

At work in the Edinburgh Royal Infirmary, 1960

A view of Aden

Some of the chaps we nursed

Bearers and sweepers outside the officers' mess

Sister and patients outside the guardroom

Sisters' mess 1965 to 1966

Anne with the Passion Wagon, Aden, 1965

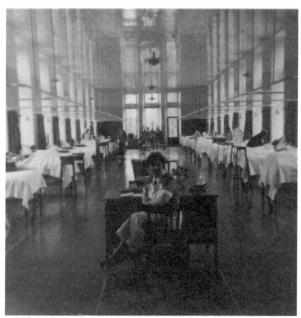

The ward

Terrorists foiled in Aden

By Clare Hollingworth

An increasing number of infiltrators is reaching Aden after having received a first-class and intensive training in terrorism and sabotage from the Egyptian-run school at Taiz, in the Southern Yemen.

The days are over when Adenis used to produce their own simple bombs and grenades, which were frequently more dangerous to the maker than anyone else.

The school at Taiz uses modern Russian detonators and time pencils, some of which were discovered by British security forces on Monday with 60lb. of plastic explosive and 14lb. of dynamite. The terrorists were apparently in the process of making this material up into bombs with meat and sweet tins.

Plastic is both easy and safe to carry around. It looks rather like ground almonds and is quite harmless in its dry condition. The noise of a plastic explosion is great in comparison with the amount of damage normally produced.

Checks and searches

There is every reason to believe terrorism is being "stepped up," although the brigadier in command of troops in Aden claims that checks and searches have foiled several terrorist plans, and at least two "killer groups" have been broken up.

Although 31 incidents have been reported in Aden during the first fortnight of July, the attacks can hardly be said to have reached dangerous proportions when compared with, say, Palestine. Only one man has been killed in Aden this year.

The railway enthusiast, Thurso to Helmsdale, September 1993

Jerusalem, 1997

Ruby wedding, 2007

Anne on the Pennine Way

Anne piloting a light aircraft, February 2020

Naomi, Michael, Charlotte and Bethany, happy grandchildren

Rory, Rosa, Fran, Ken and Anne, daughters and son-in-laws

THE ROYAL BRITISH LEGION

This Certificate

is Awarded to

Anne Bolam

**as a mark of esteem
and appreciation of her outstanding service to
The Royal British Legion
West Reading Branch**

President

Michael Furness   *Chairman*

Mary Pelcher   *Secretary*

The Royal County of Berkshire

16|10|07